Enjoy!!!

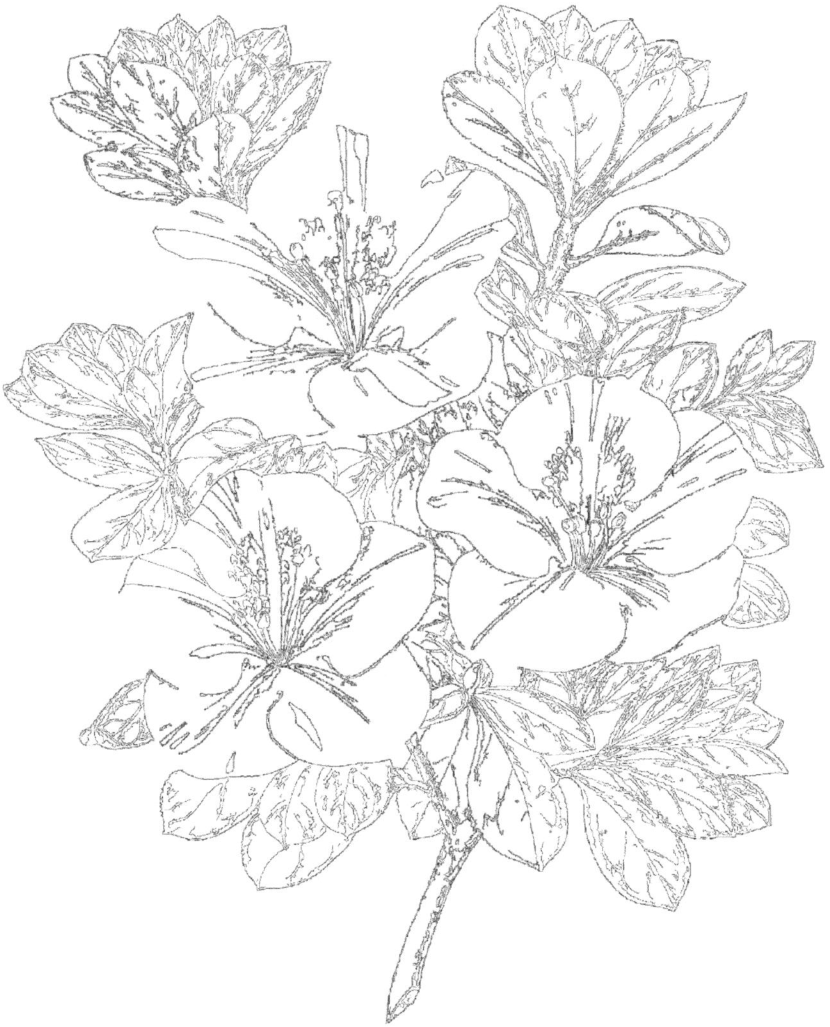

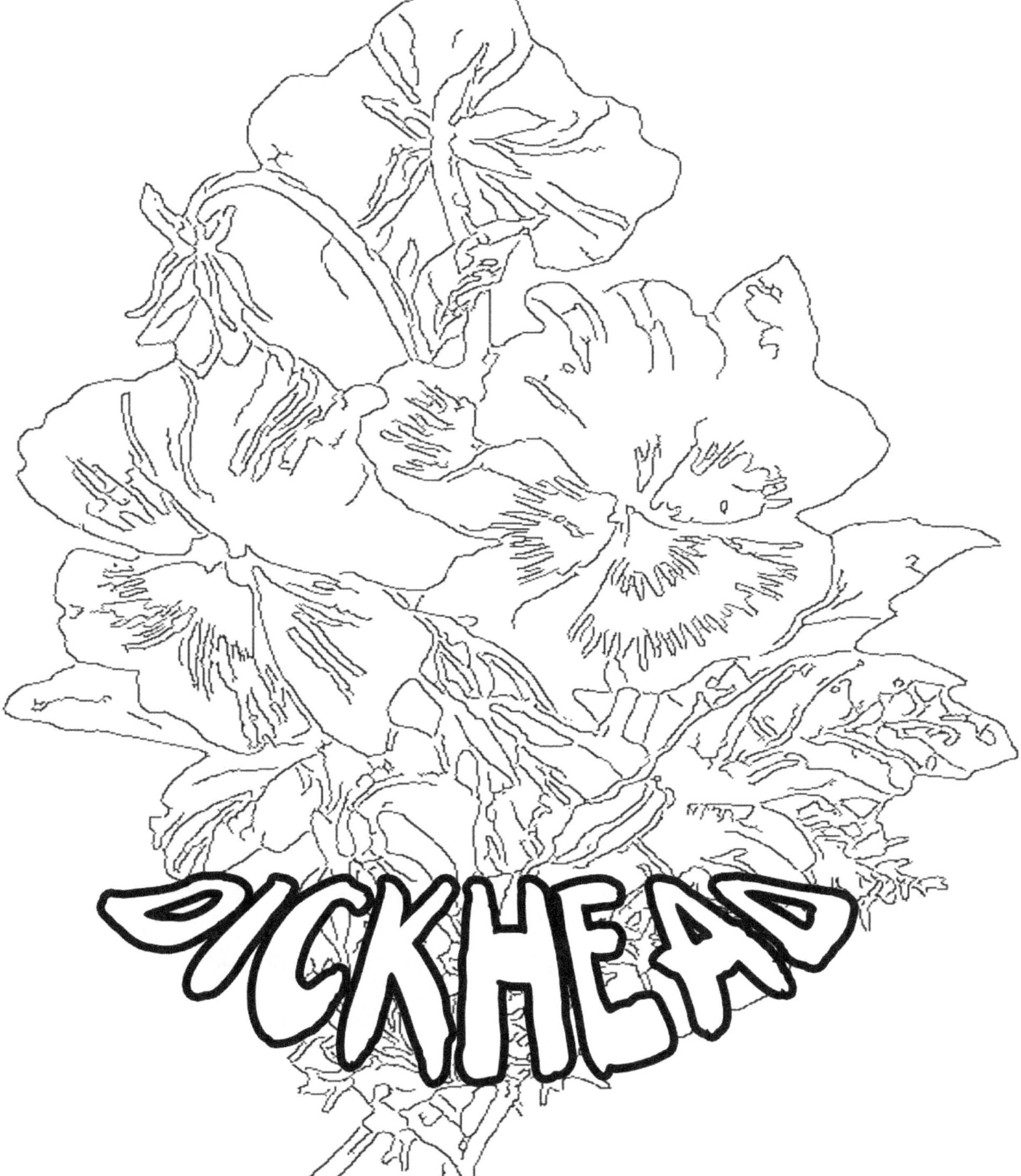
DICKHEAD

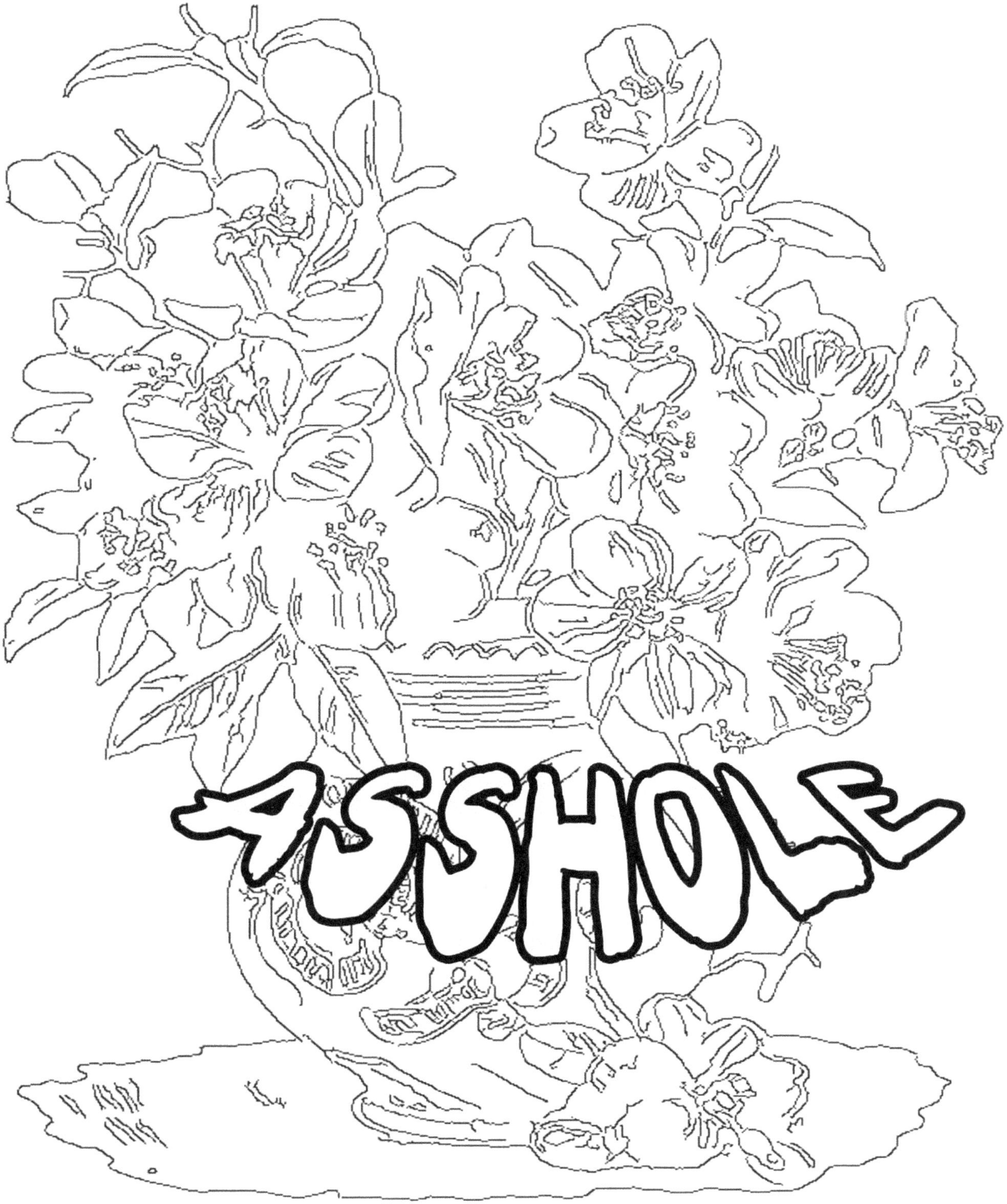
ASSHOLE

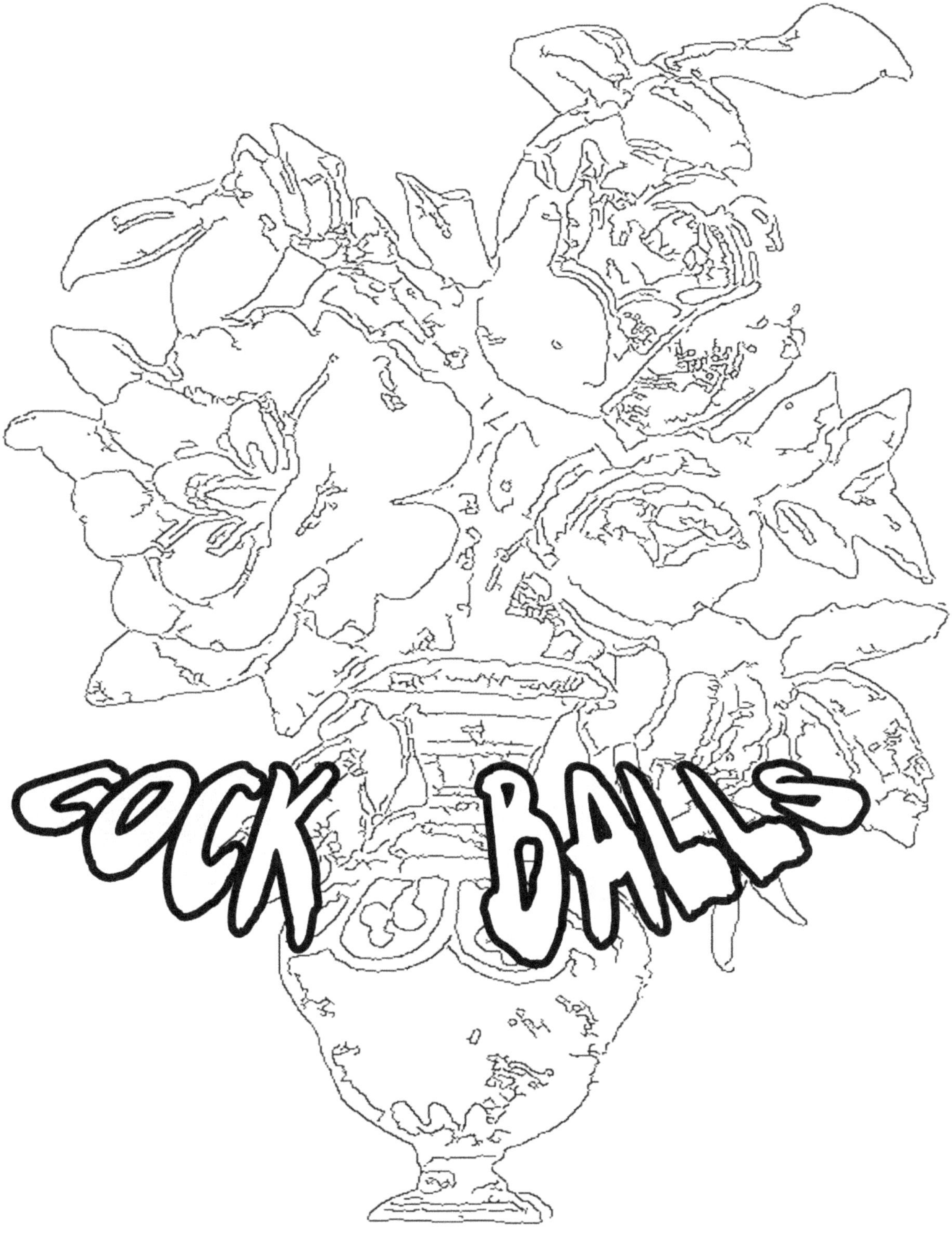
COCK BALLS

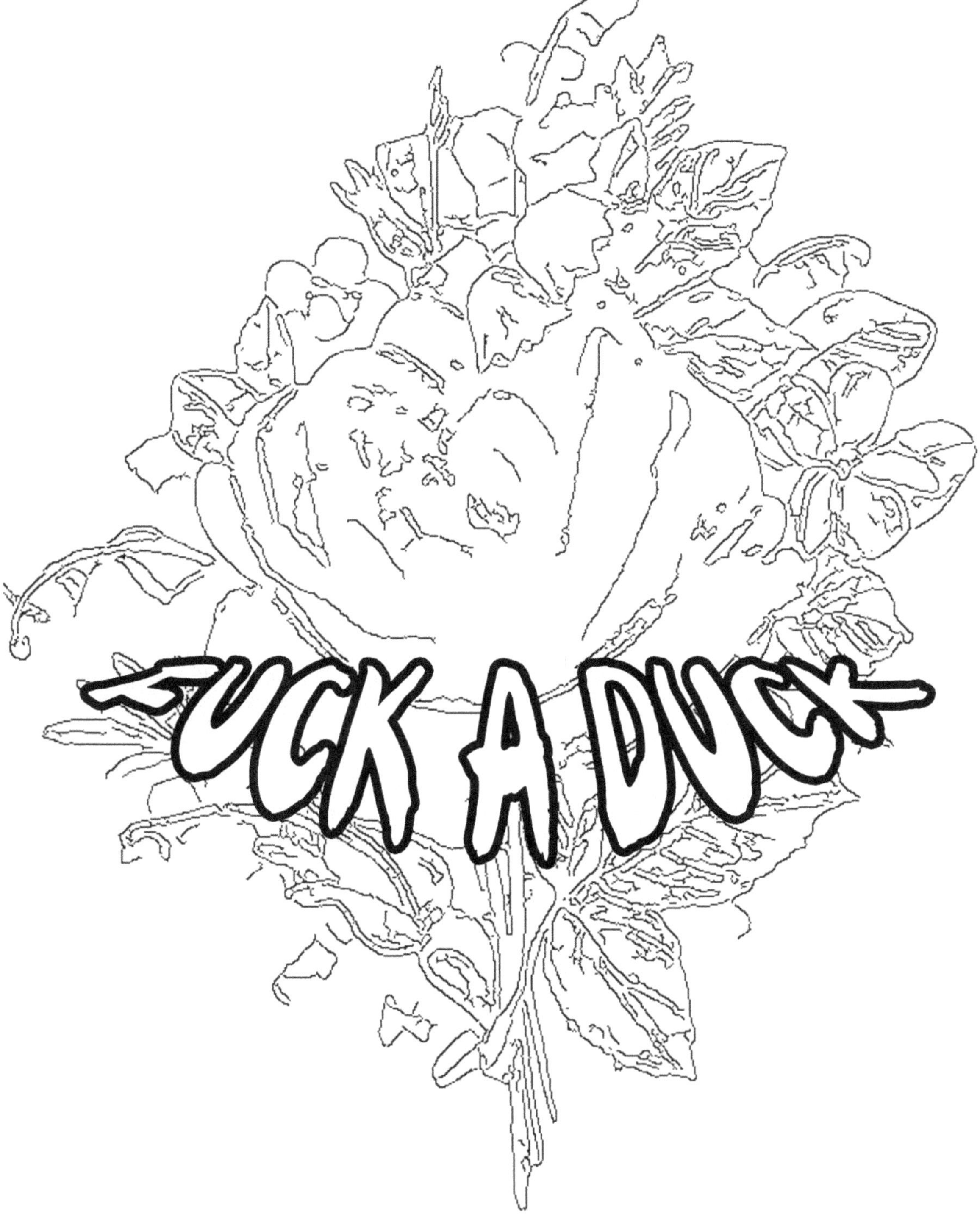
FUCK A DUCK

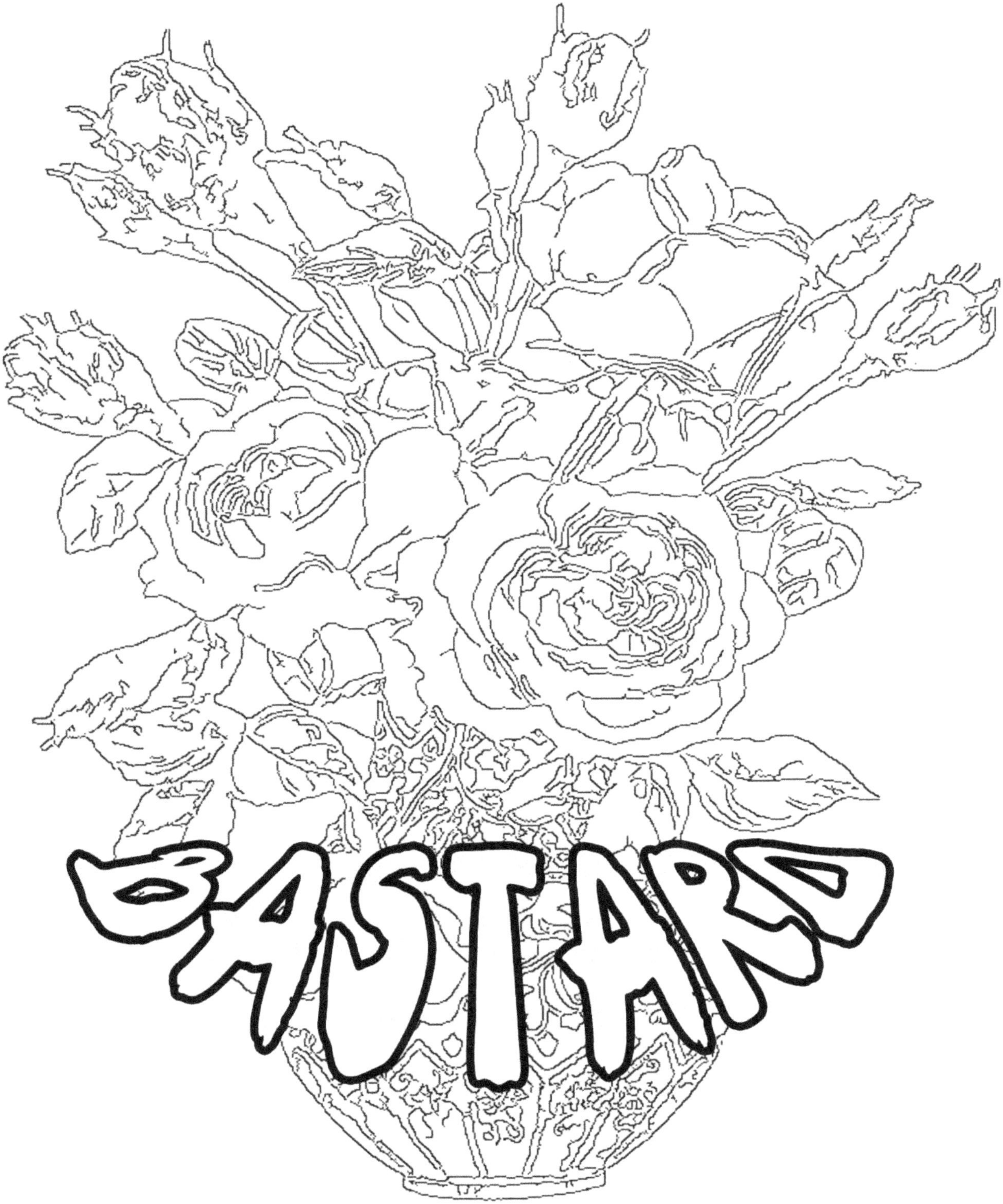
BASTARD

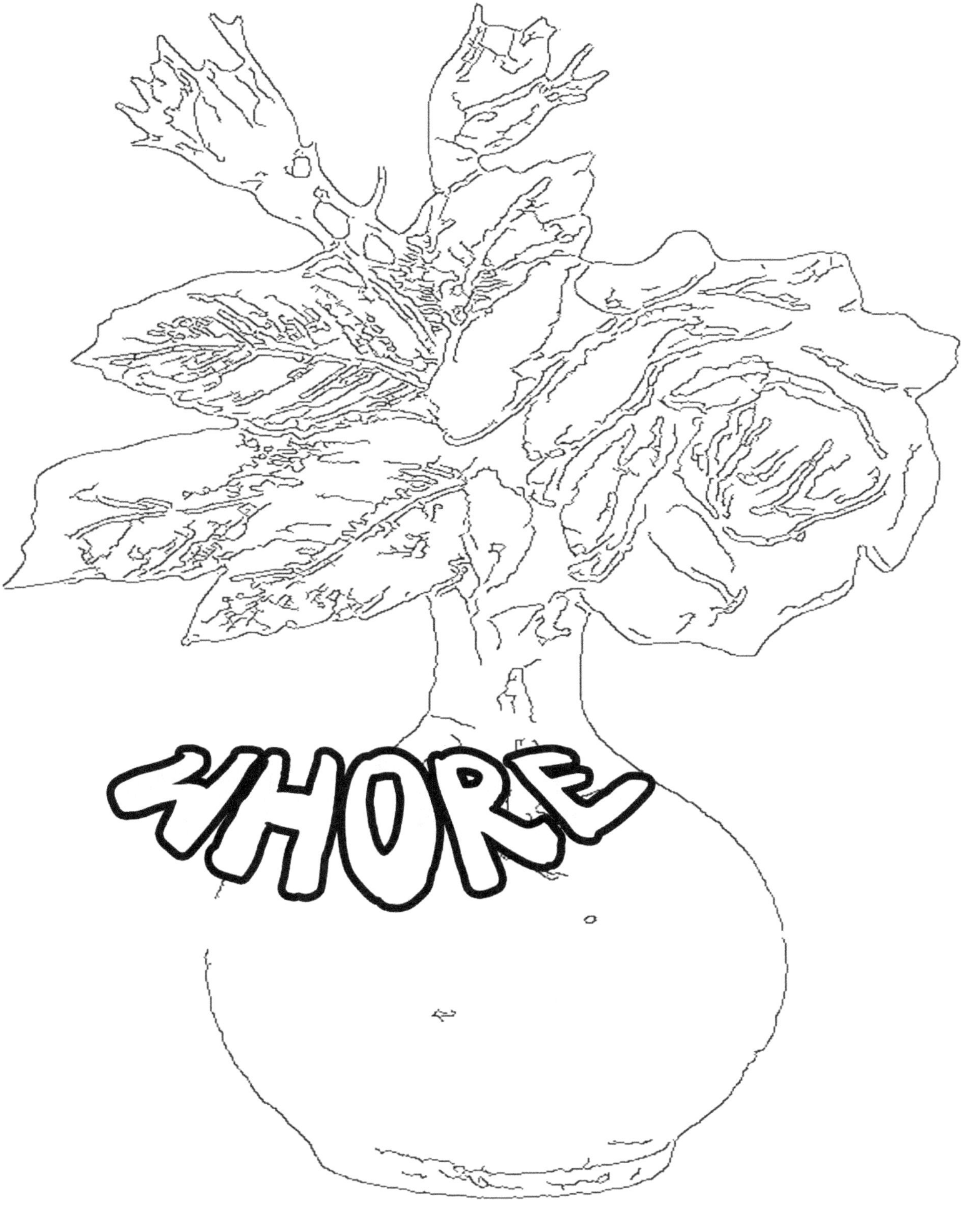
WHORE

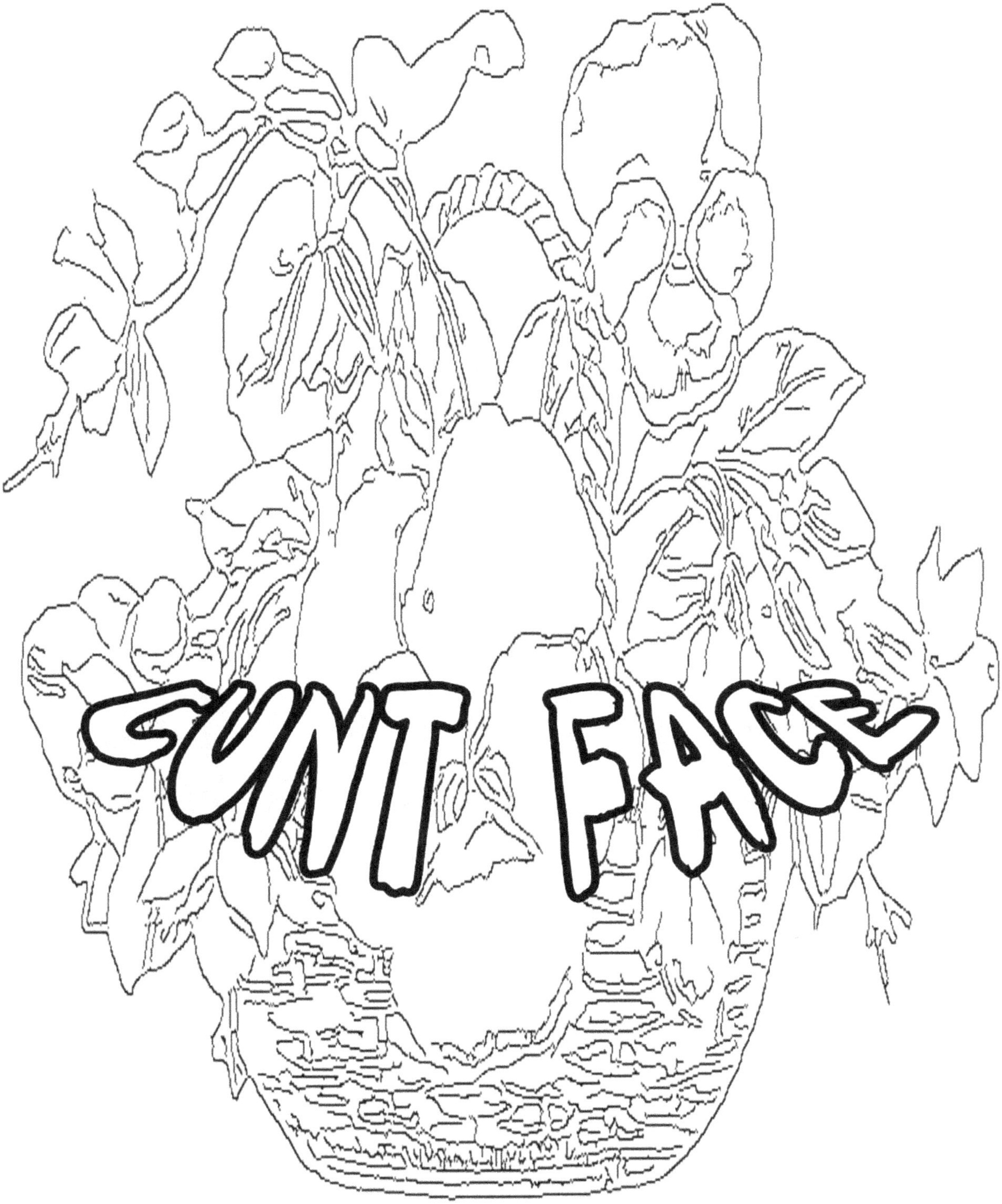
CUNT FACE

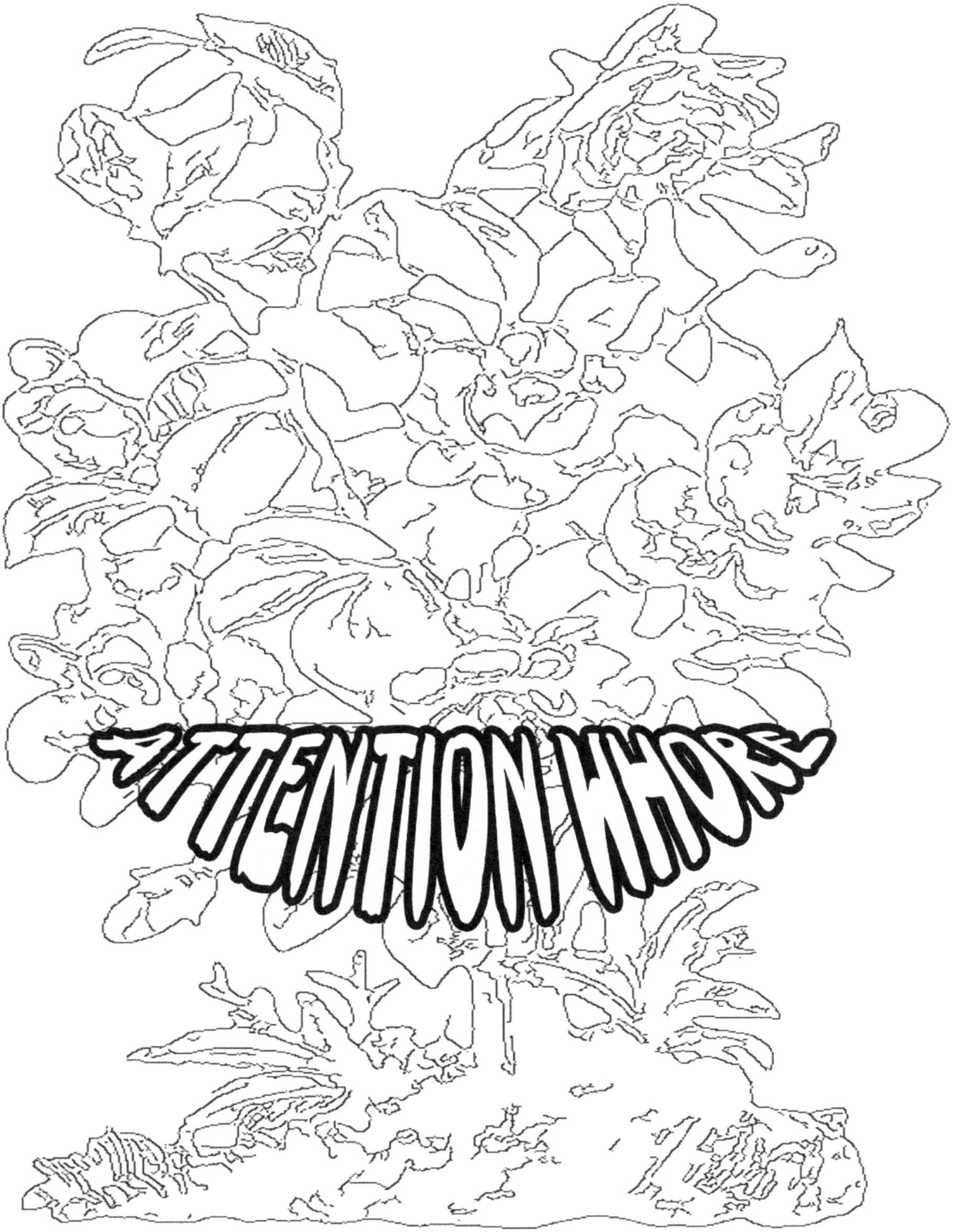
ATTENTION WHORE

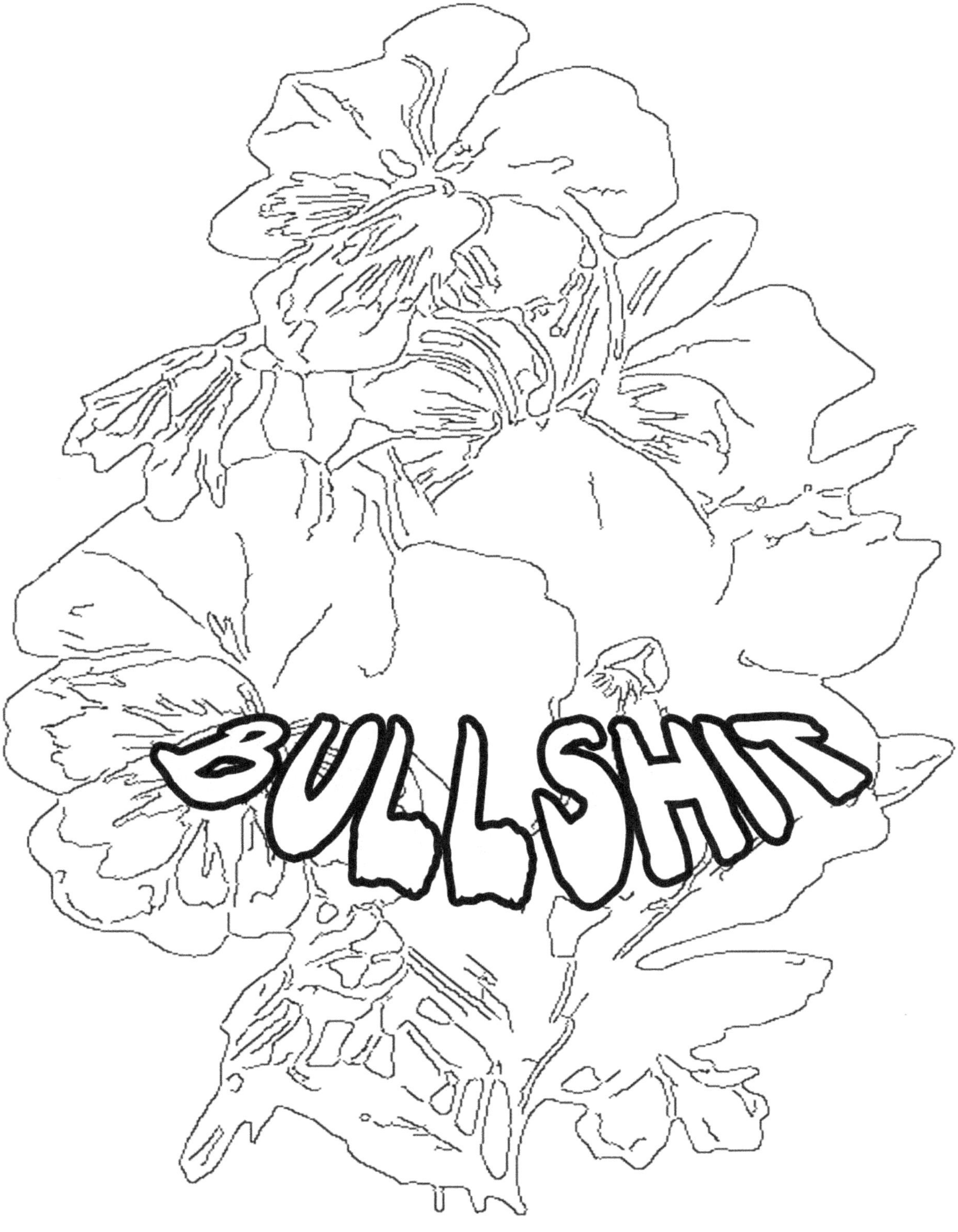
BULLSHIT

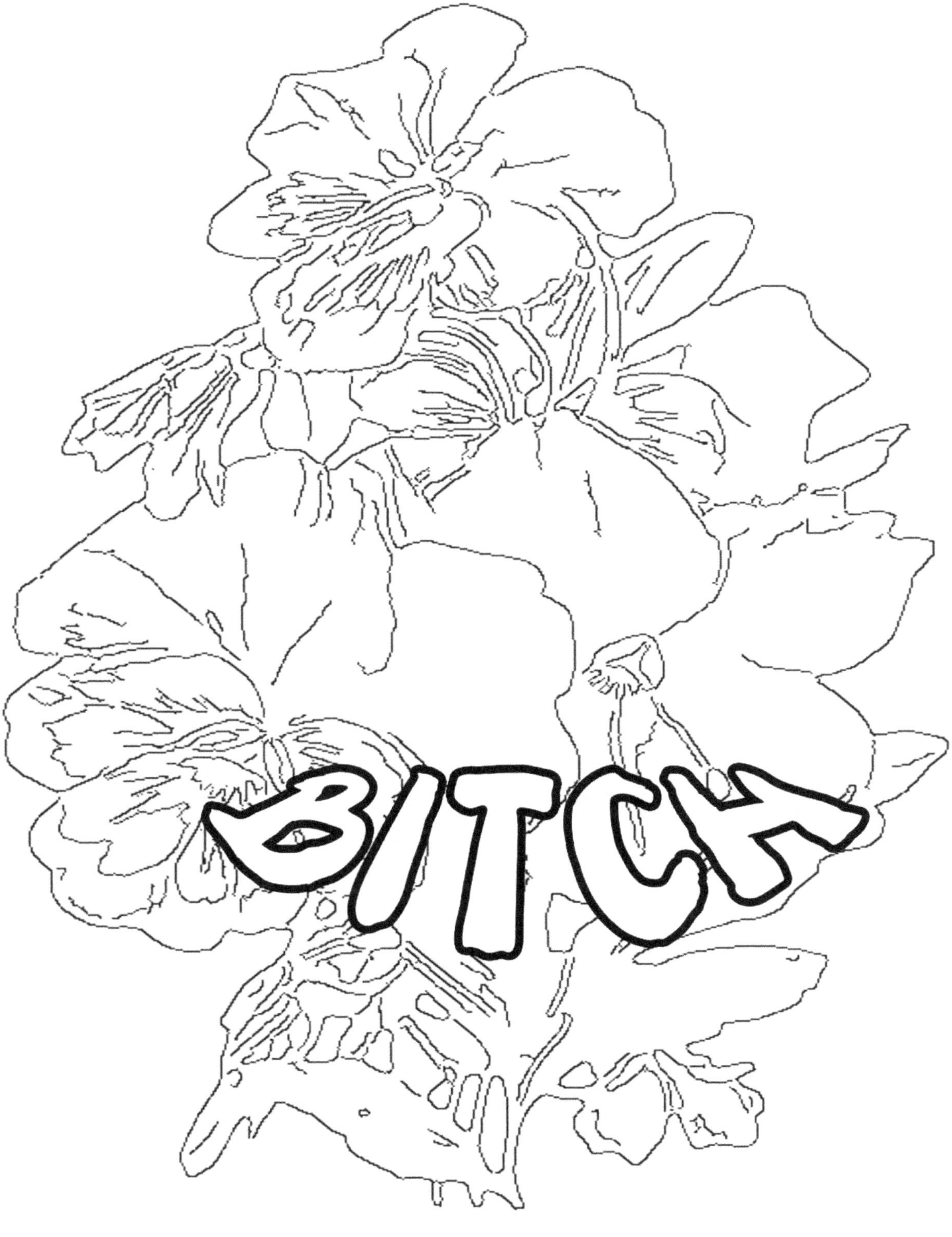
BITCH

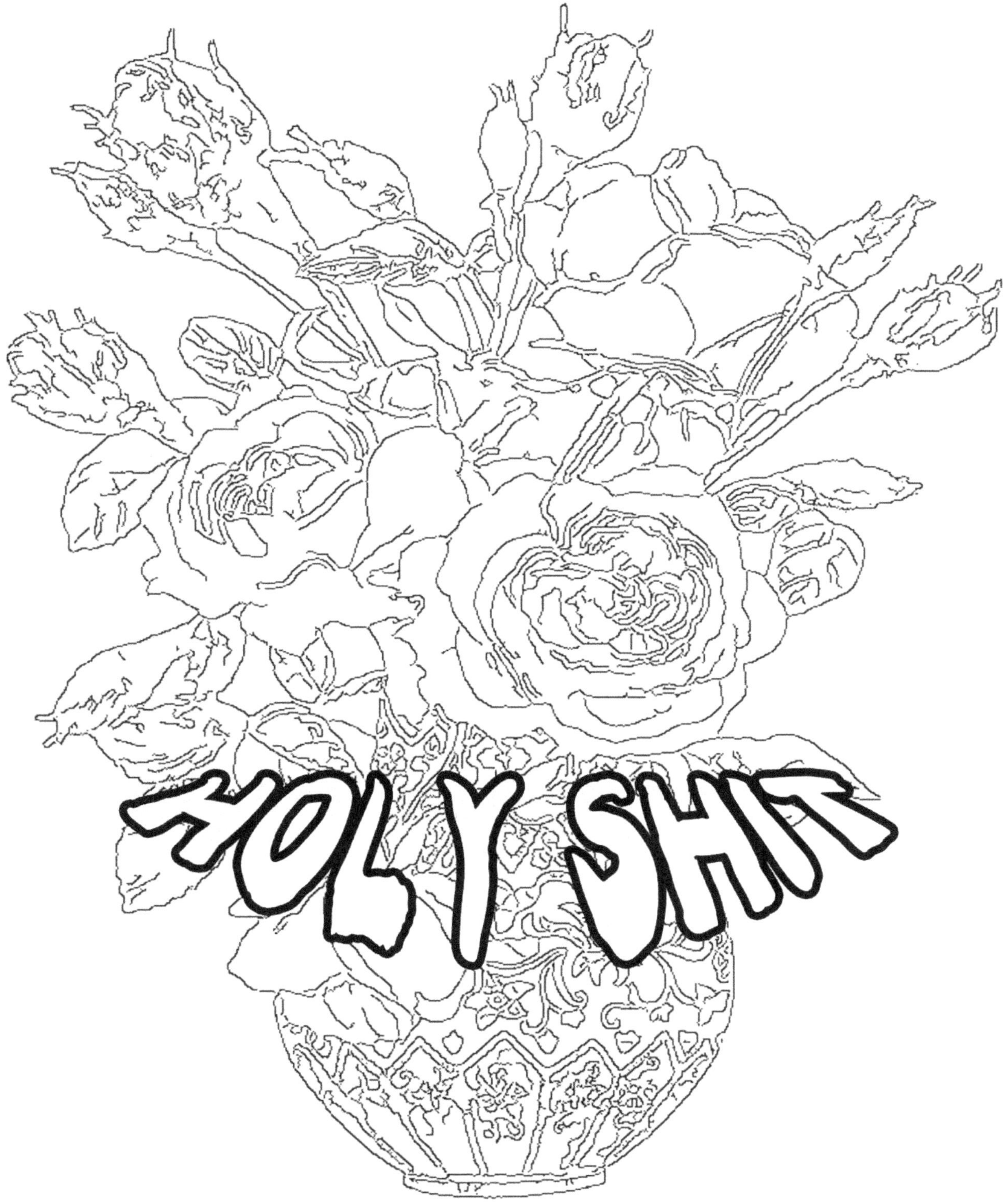
HOLY SHIT

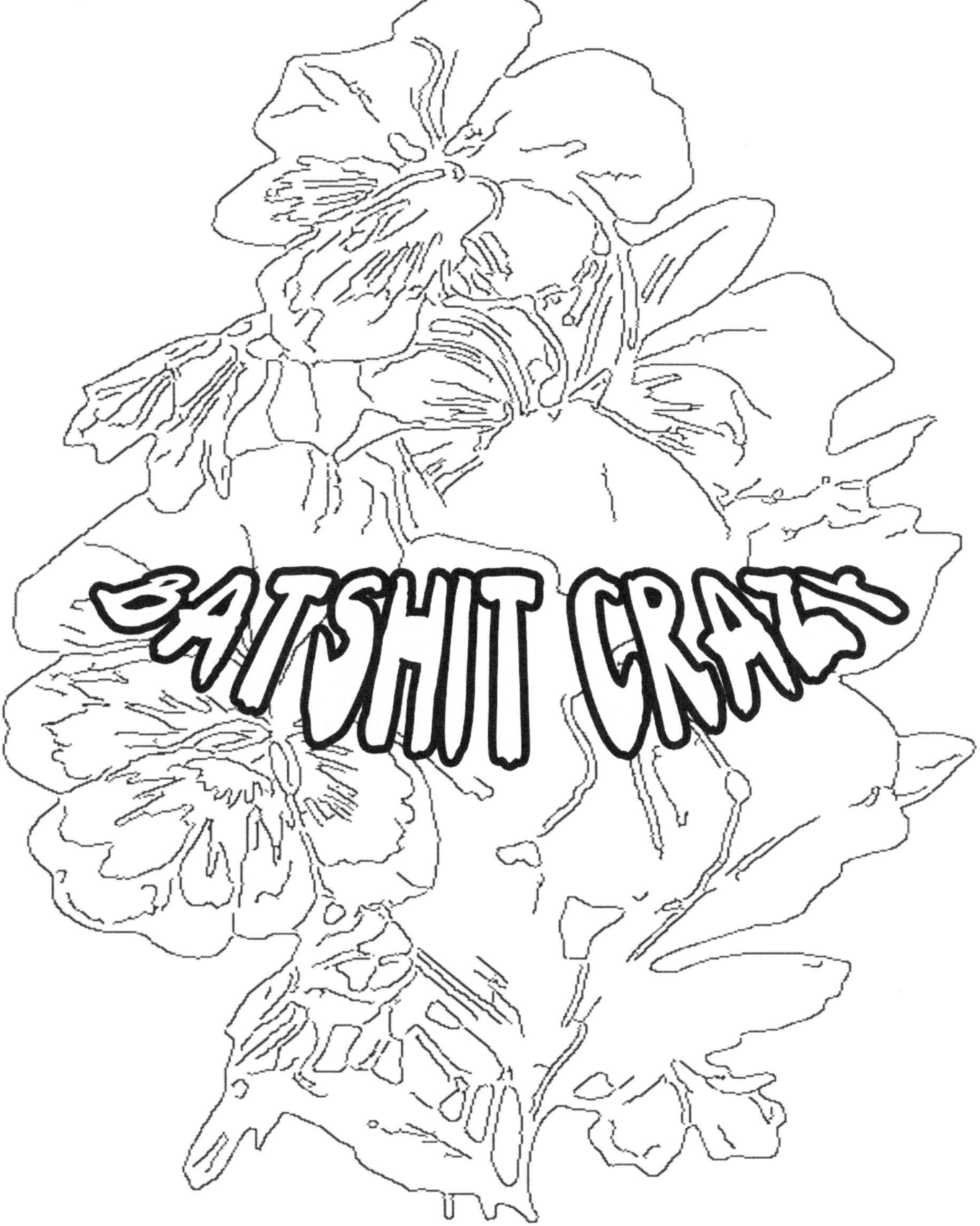
BATSHIT CRAZY

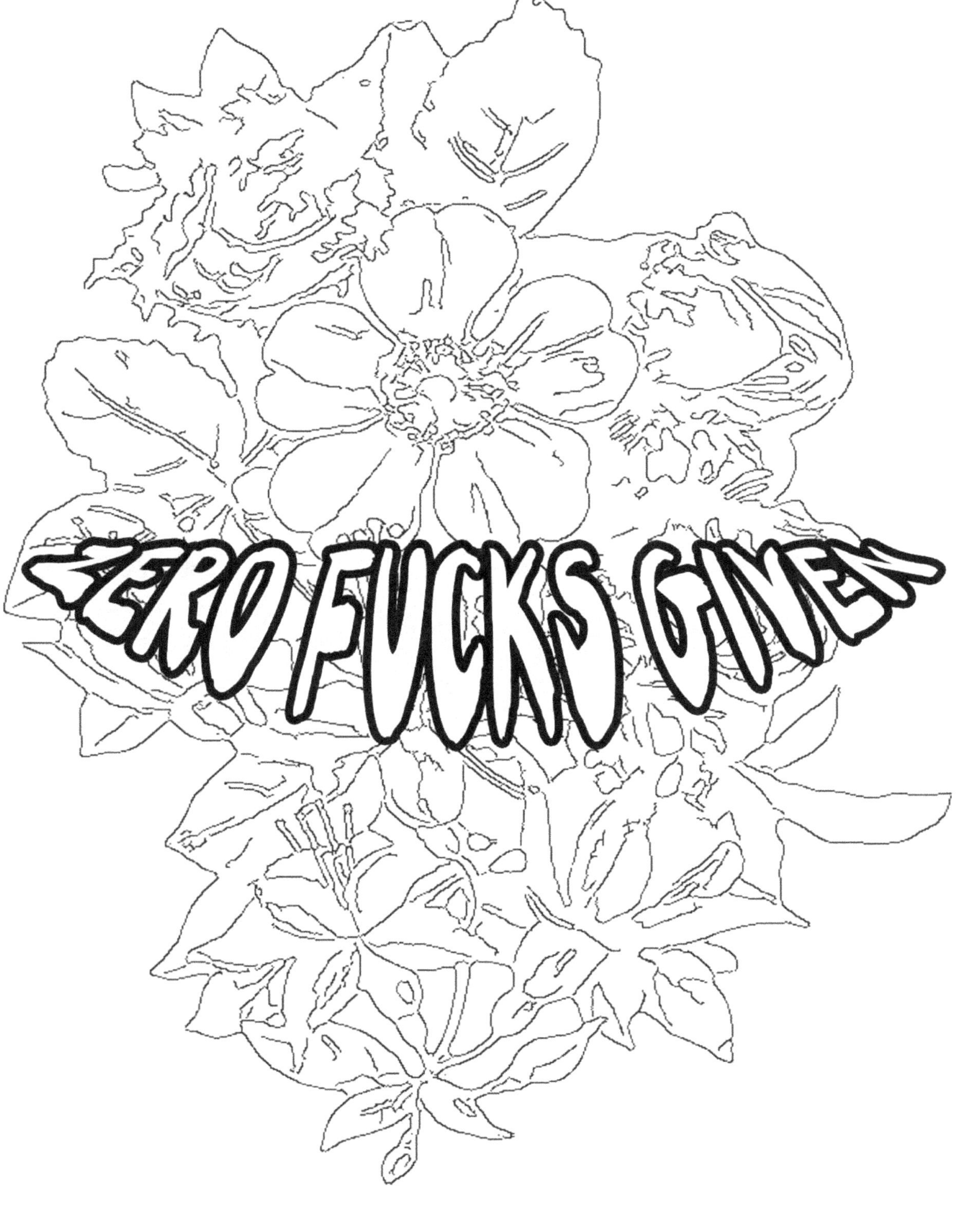
ZERO FUCKS GIVEN

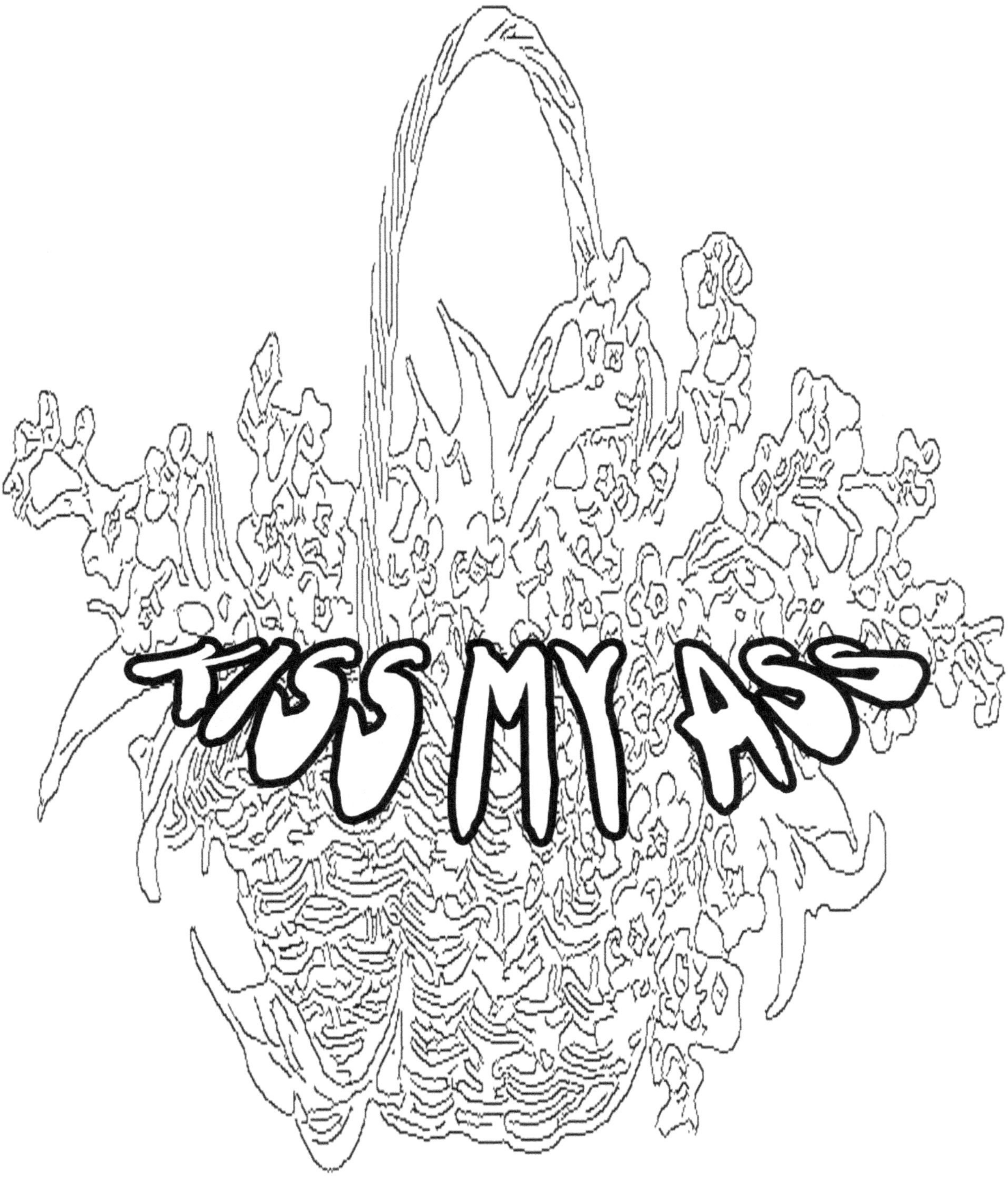
KISS MY ASS

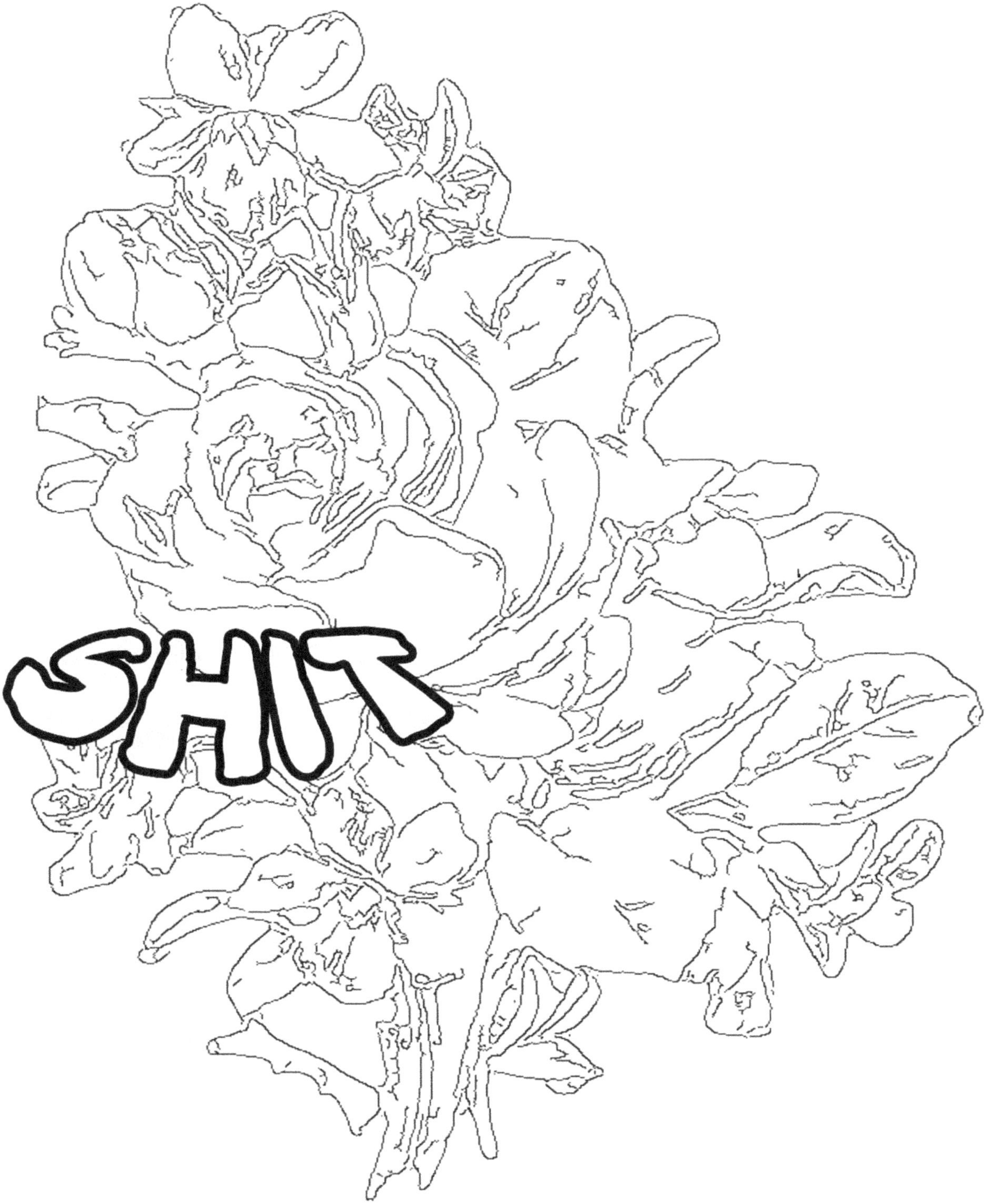
SHIT

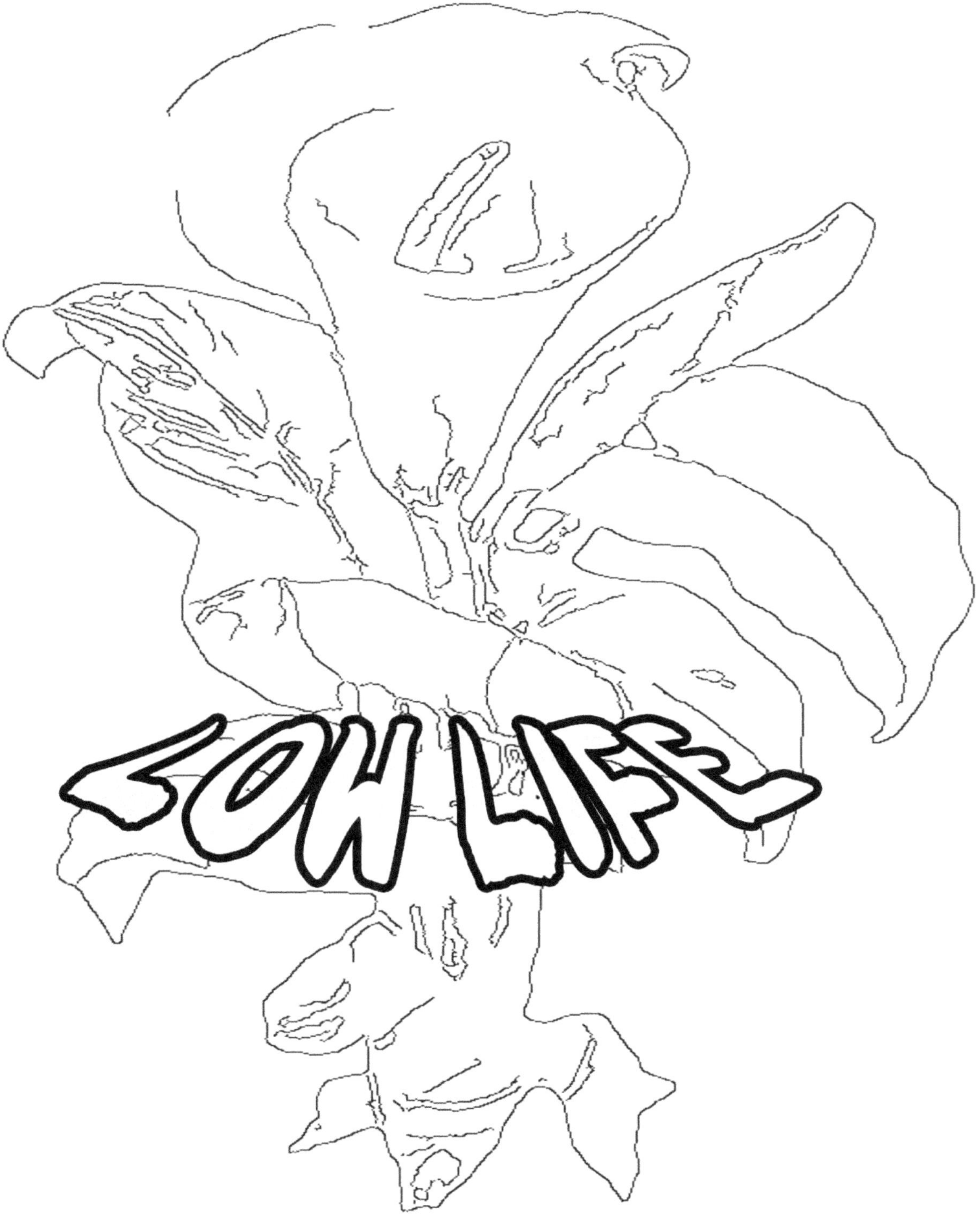
LOW LIFE

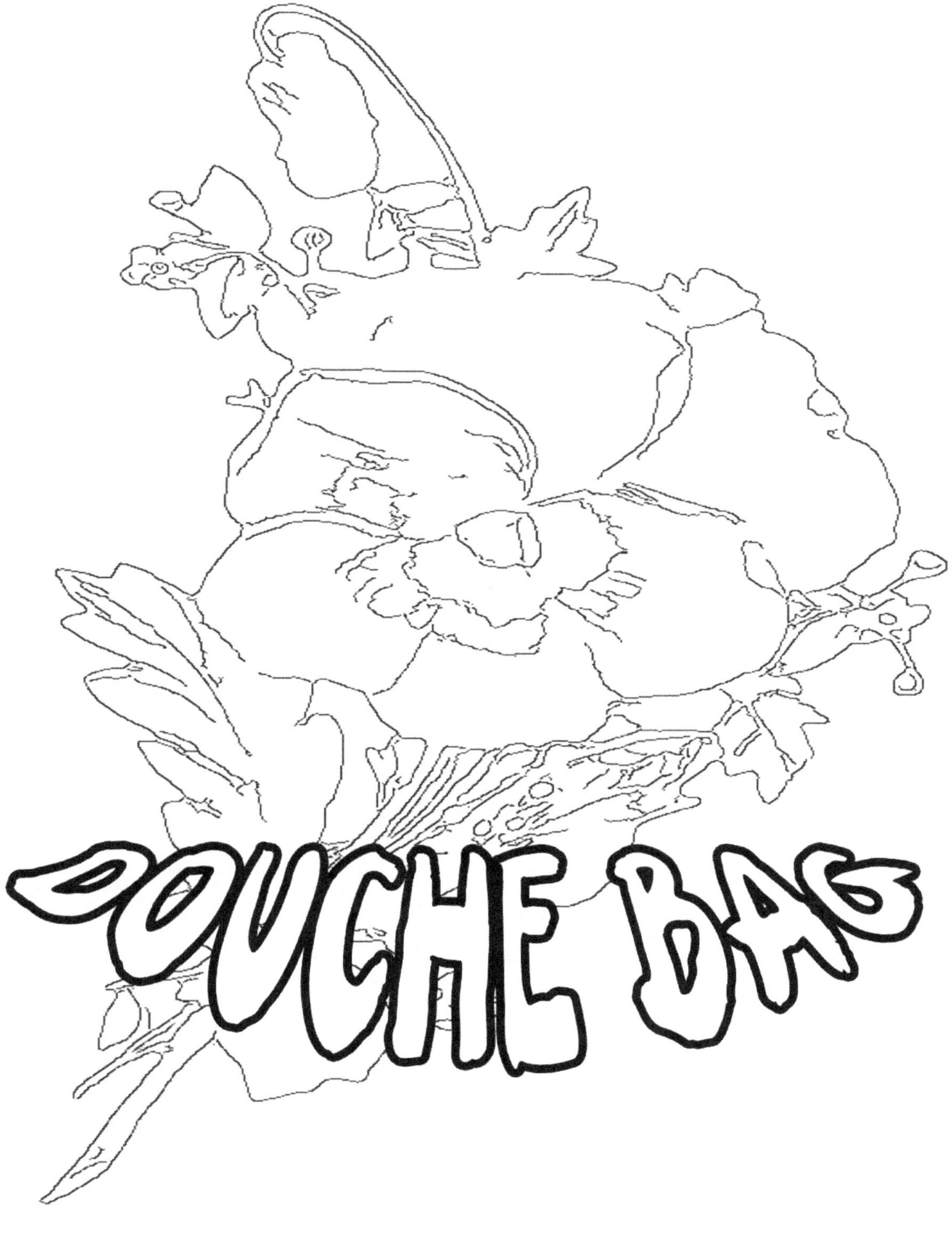
DOUCHE BAG

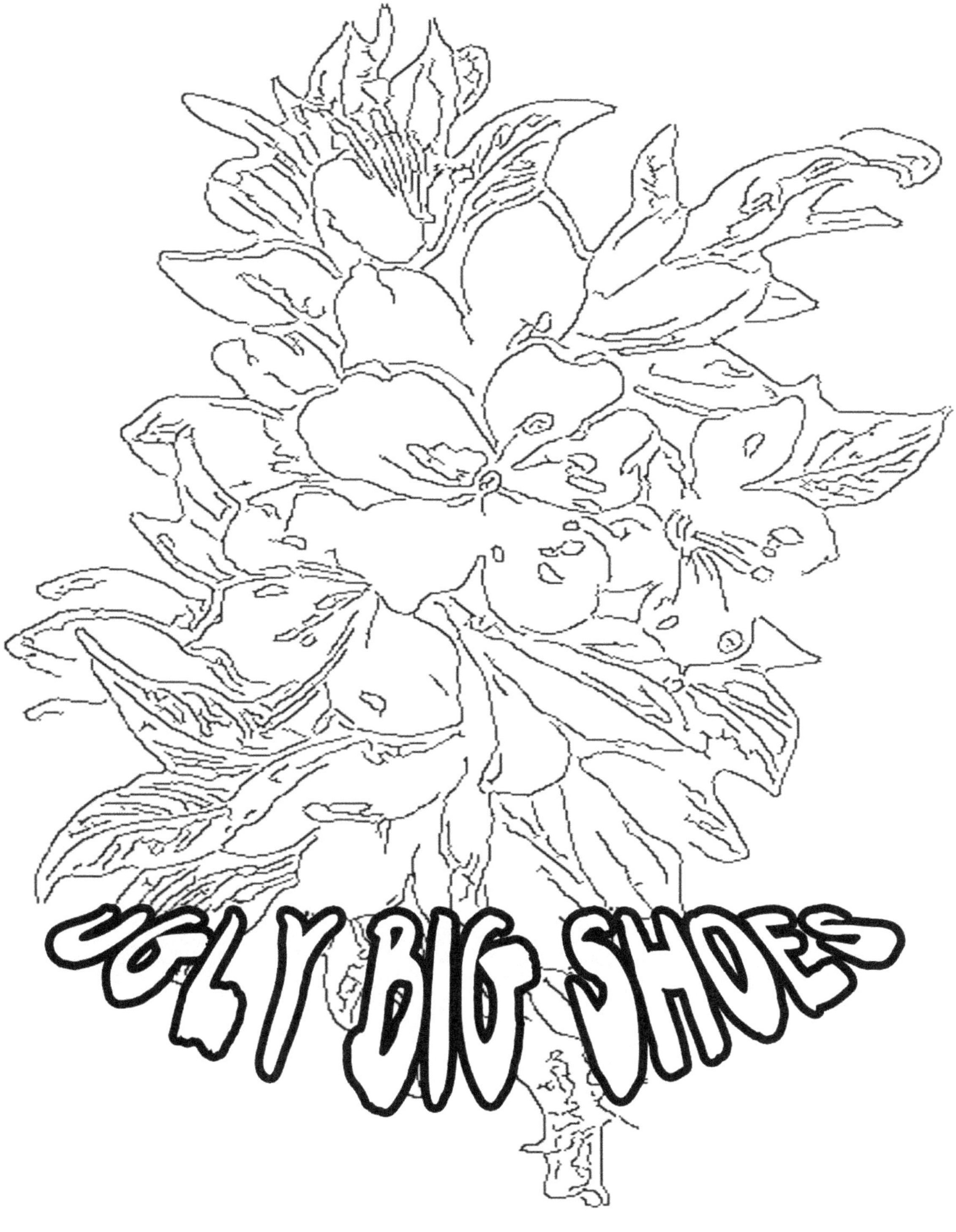
UGLY BIG SHOES

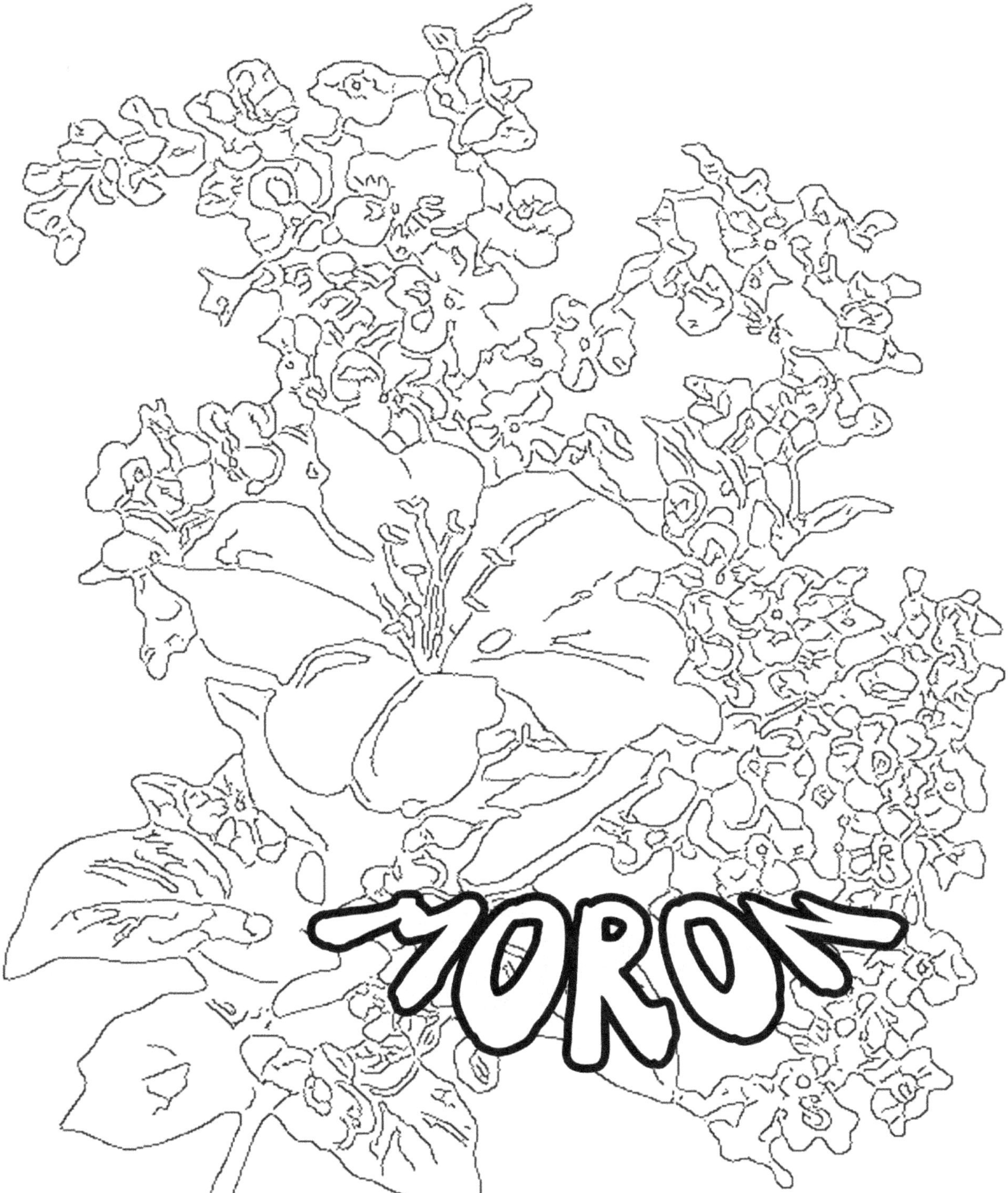
MORON

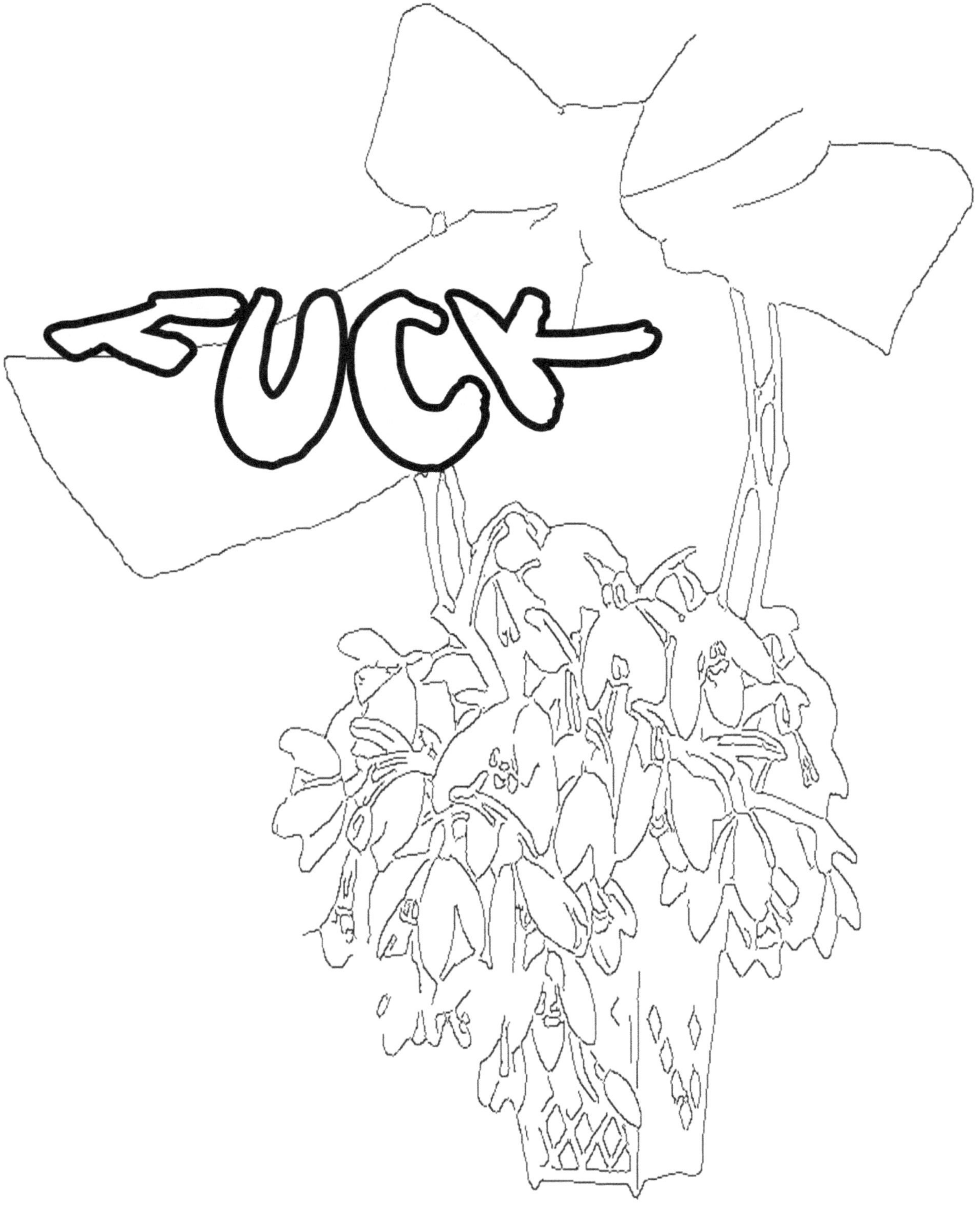
FUCK

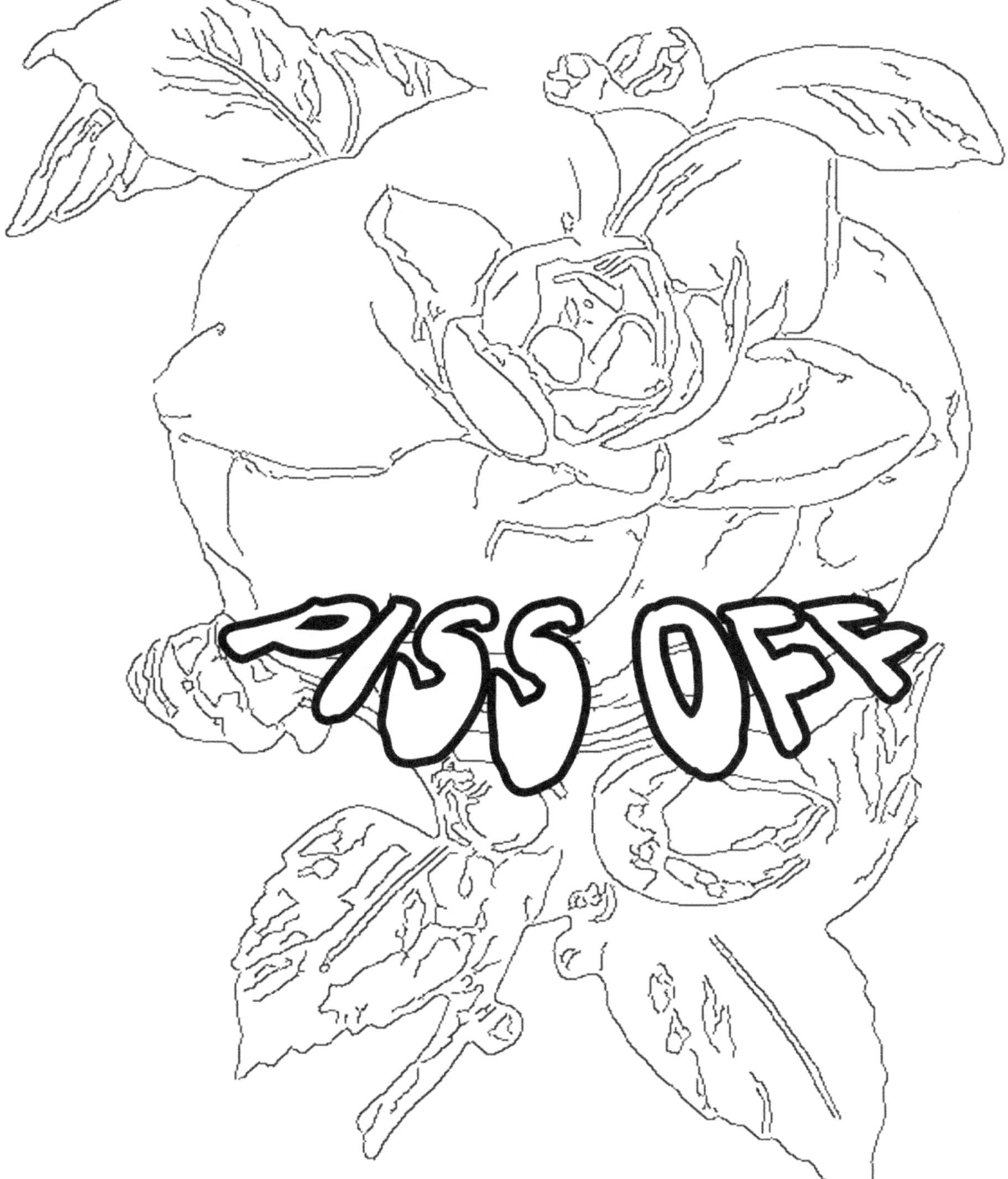
PISS OFF

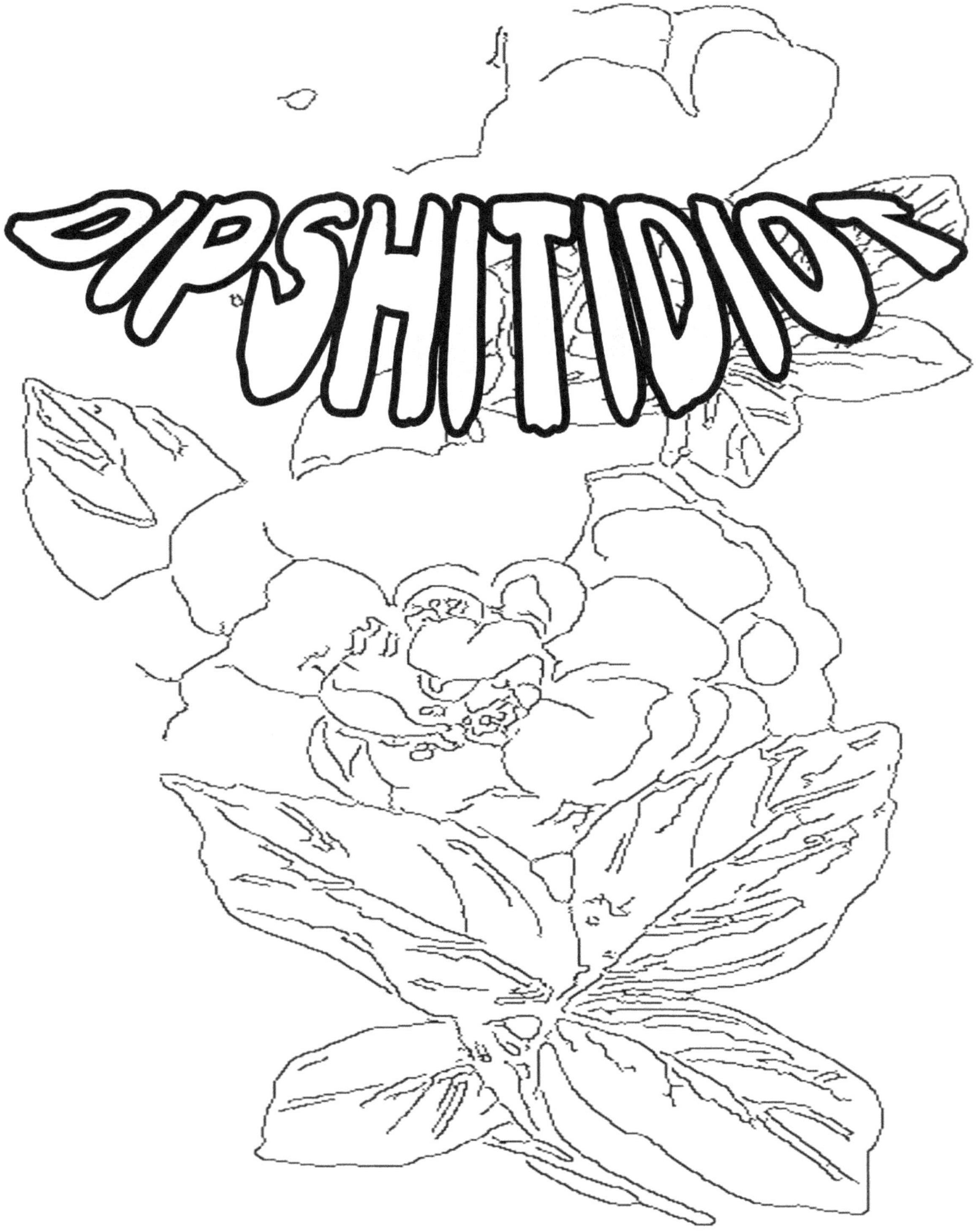
DIPSHITIDIOT

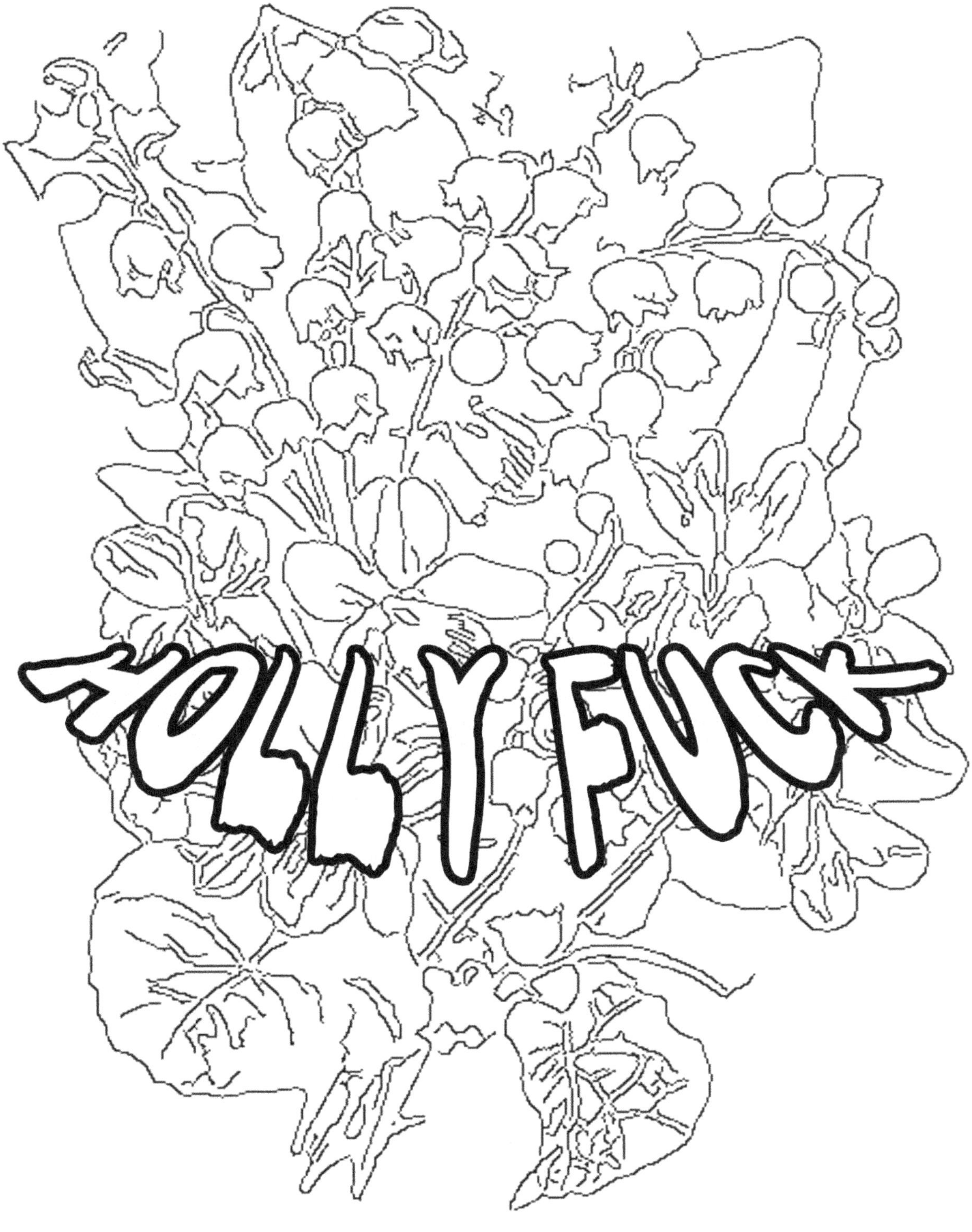
HOLLY FUCK

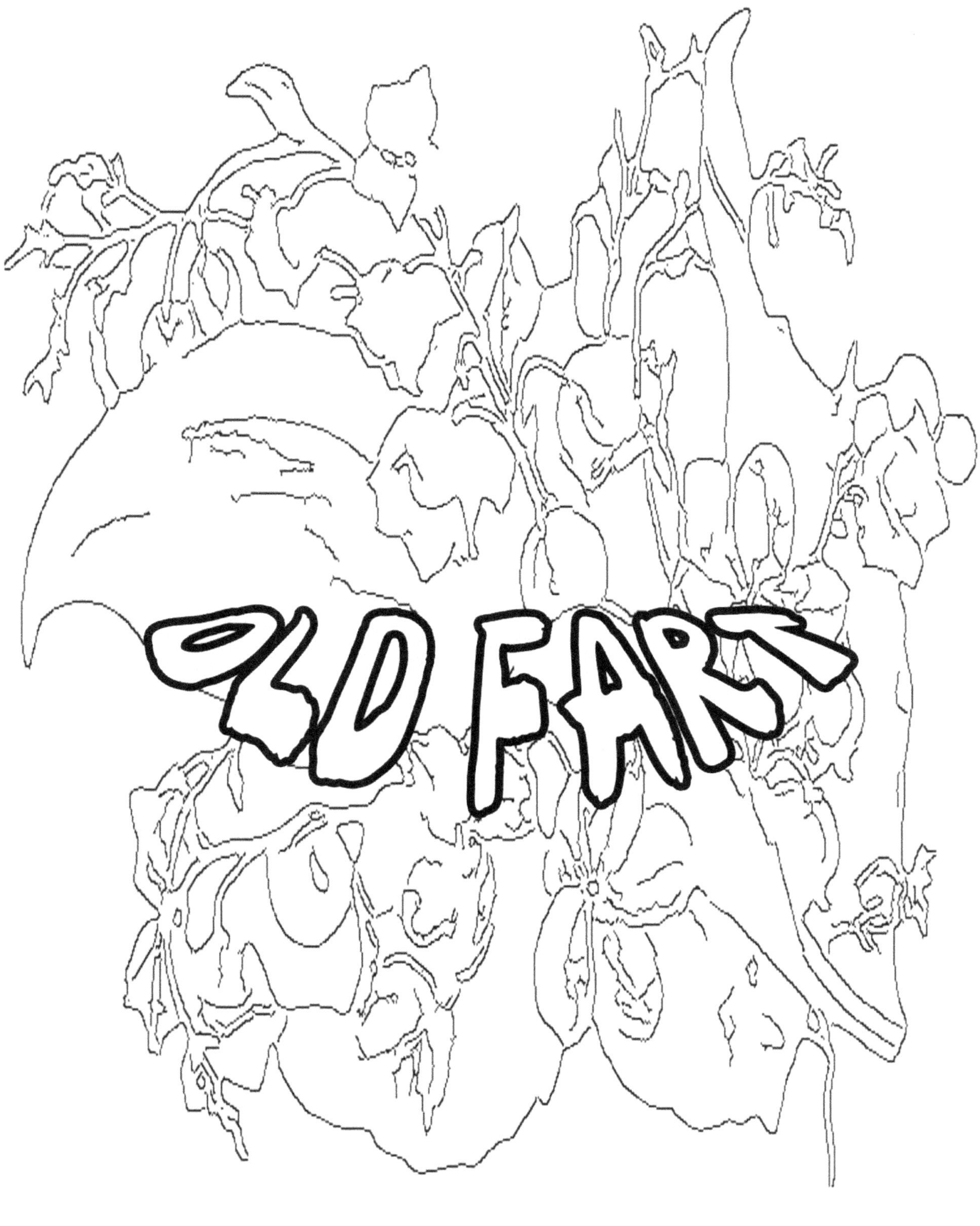
OLD FART

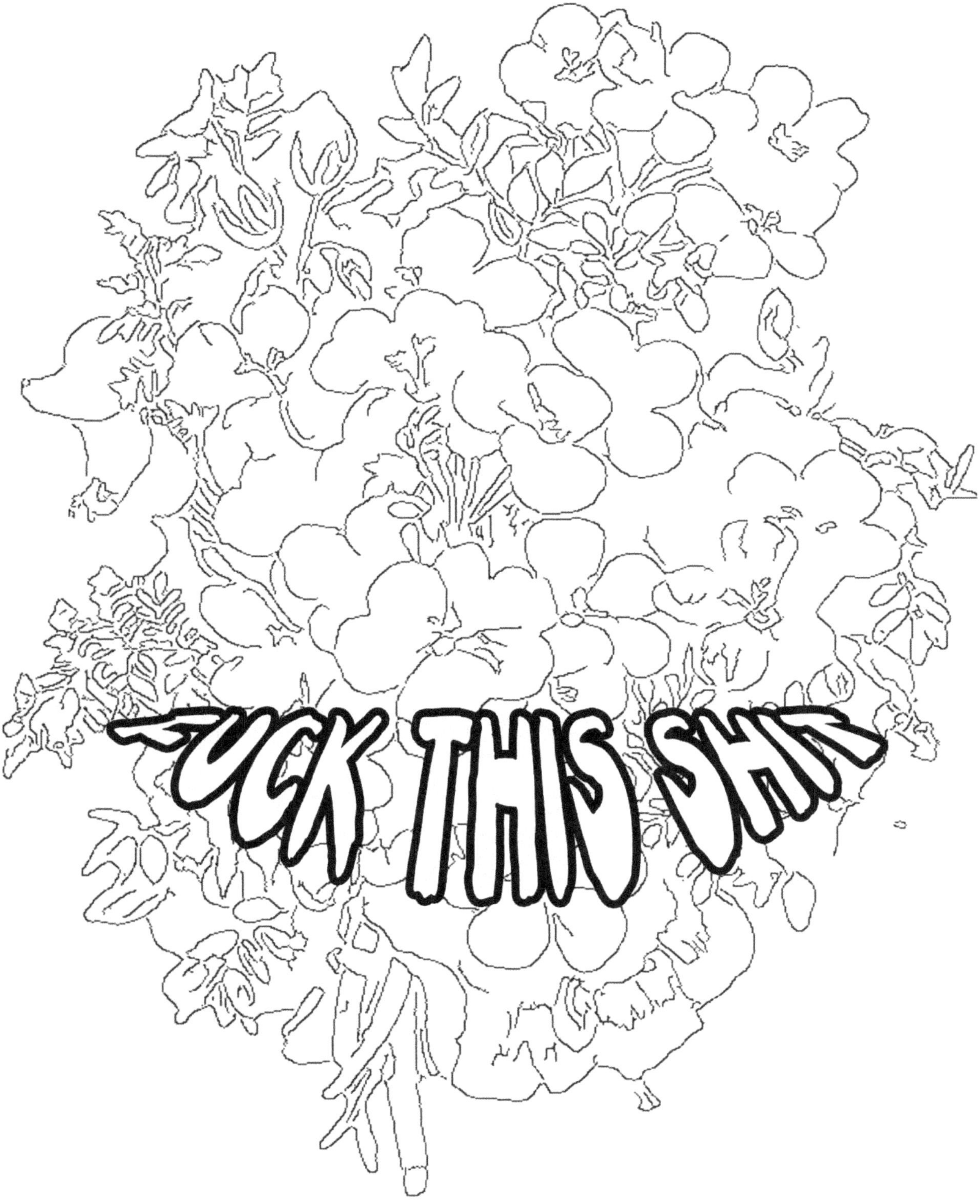
UCK THIS SHI

Have a good day.

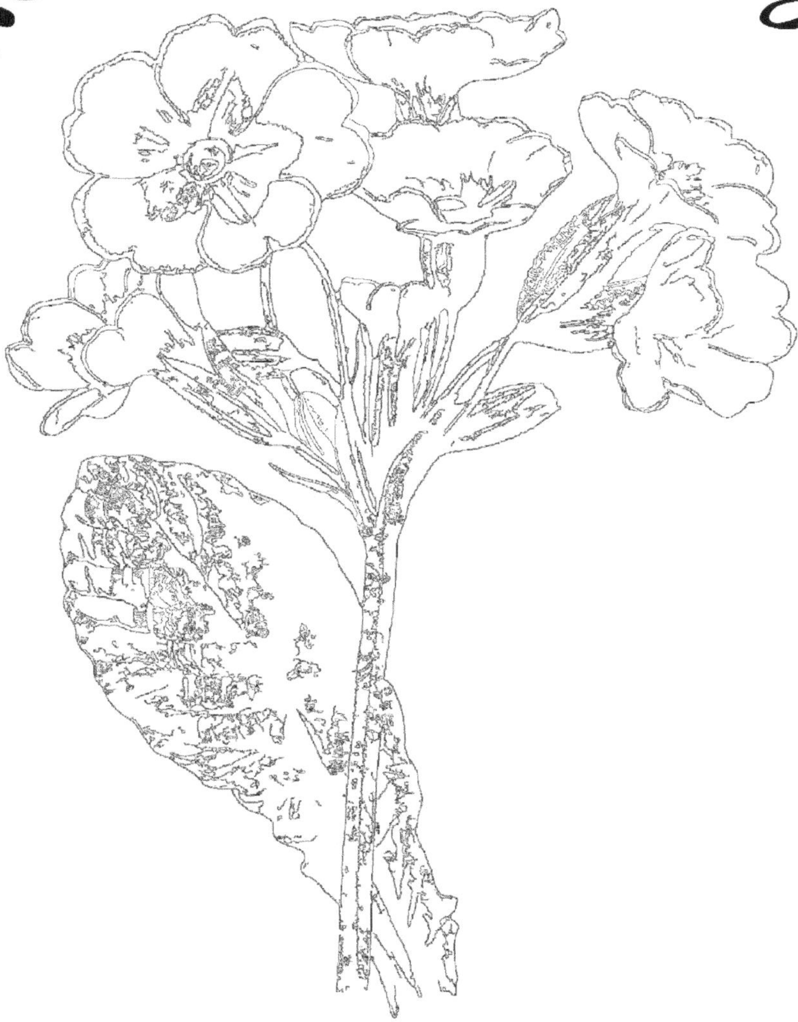

www.ingramcontent.com/pod-product-compliance
Lightning Source LLC
Chambersburg PA
CBHW081620220526
45468CB00010B/2956